Life History of Floyd Mayweather Jr.

ISBN-13: 978-1975809478

Contents

Floyd Joy Mayweather Jr

Floyd Joy Mayweather Jr. (born **Floyd Joy Sinclair**; February 24, 1977) is an American professional boxer and promoter. Mayweather is undefeated in his professional boxing career and a five-division world champion, having won fifteen world titles and the lineal championship in four different weight classes (twice at welterweight). As an amateur he won a bronze medal in the featherweight division at the 1996 Olympics, three U.S. Golden Gloves championships (at light flyweight, flyweight, and featherweight), and the U.S. national championship at featherweight.

Mayweather is a two-time winner of *The Ring* magazine's Fighter of the Year award (1998 and 2007), a three-time winner of the Boxing Writers Association of America Fighter of the Year award (2007, 2013, and 2015), and a six-time winner of the Best Fighter ESPY Award (2007–2010, 2012–2014) In 2016, Mayweather was ranked by ESPN as the greatest boxer, pound for pound, of the last 25 years. In the same year, he peaked as BoxRec's number one fighter of all time, pound for pound, as well as the greatest welterweight of all time.[5][6] Many sporting news and boxing websites, including *The Ring*, *Sports Illustrated*, ESPN, BoxRec, Fox Sports, and Yahoo! Sports, ranked Mayweather as the best pound for pound boxer in the world twice in a span of ten years.

He is often referred to as the best defensive boxer in history, as well as being the most accurate puncher since the existence of CompuBox, having the highest plus–minus ratio in recorded boxing history. As of his most recent fight in 2015, Mayweather has a record of 26 wins without a loss or draw in world title fights (10 by KO), 23 wins (9 KOs) in lineal title fights, 24 wins (7 KOs) against former or current world titlists, 12 wins (3 KOs) against former or current lineal champions, and 2 wins (1 KO) against International Boxing Hall of Fame inductees.

In addition to his accomplishments in the ring, Mayweather is well known for being one of the most lucrative pay-per-view (PPV) attractions of all time, in any sport. He topped the *Forbes* and *Sports Illustrated* lists of the 50 highest-paid athletes of 2012 and 2013 respectively, and the *Forbes* list again in both 2014 and 2015 listing him as the highest paid athlete in the world. In 2007 he founded his own boxing promotional firm, Mayweather Promotions, after defecting from Bob Arum's Top Rank.[Mayweather has generated approximately 19.5 million in PPV buys and $1.3 billion in revenue throughout his career, surpassing the likes of former top PPV attractions including Mike Tyson, Evander Holyfield, Lennox Lewis, Oscar De La Hoya, and Manny Pacquiao.[

Statistics

Real name	Floyd Joy Mayweather Jr.
Nickname(s)	<ul><li>Pretty Boy</li><li>Money</li></ul>
Weight(s)	<ul><li>Super featherweight</li><li>Lightweight</li><li>Light welterweight</li><li>Welterweight</li><li>Light middleweight</li></ul>
Height	5 ft 8 in (173 cm)
Reach	72 in (183 cm)
Nationality	American
Born	Floyd Joy Sinclair February 24, 1977 (age 40) Grand Rapids, Michigan, U.S.
Stance	Orthodox

Boxing record

Total fights	49
Wins	49
Wins by KO	26
Losses	0

Medal record[hide]

Men's amateur boxing

Representing ▄ United States

Olympic Games		
Ⓑ	1996 Atlanta	Featherweigh

Early life and education

Mayweather was born in Grand Rapids, Michigan, on February 24, 1977, into a family of boxers. His father, Floyd Mayweather Sr., was a former welterweight contender who fought Hall of Famer Sugar Ray Leonard. His uncles (Jeff Mayweather and Roger Mayweather) were professional boxers, with Roger – Floyd's former trainer – winning two world championships, fought Hall of Famers Julio César Chávez, Pernell Whitaker and Kostya Tszyu. Mayweather was born with his mother's last name, but his last name would change to Mayweather shortly thereafter. Mayweather attended Ottawa Hills High School before he dropped out.

Floyd Mayweather Jr., His father, Floyd Mayweather Sr.,

Boxing has been a part of Mayweather's life since his childhood and he never seriously considered any other profession. "I think my grandmother saw my potential first," Mayweather said. "When I was young, I told her 'I think I should get a job.' She said, 'No, just keep boxing'." "When I was about eight or nine, I lived in New Jersey with my mother and we were seven deep in one bedroom and sometimes we didn't have electricity." Mayweather said. "When people see what I have now, they have no idea of where I came from and how I didn't have anything growing up."

It was not uncommon for young Mayweather to come home from school and find used heroin needles in his front yard. His mother was addicted to drugs, and he had an aunt who died from AIDS because of her drug use. "People don't know the hell I've been through," he says.

The most time that his father spent with him was taking him to the gym to train and work on his boxing, according to Mayweather. "I don't remember him ever taking me anywhere or doing anything that a father would do with a son, going to the park or to the movies or to get ice cream," he says. "I always thought that he liked his daughter (Floyd's older sister) better than he liked me because she never got whippings and I got whippings all the time."

Mayweather's father contends that Floyd is not telling the truth about their early relationship. "Even though his daddy did sell drugs, I didn't deprive my son," the elder Mayweather says. "The drugs I sold, he was a part of it. He had plenty of food. He had the best clothes and I gave him money. He didn't want for anything. Anybody in Grand Rapids can tell you that I took care of my kids". Floyd Sr. says he did all of his hustling at night and spent his days with his son, taking him to the gym and training him to be a boxer. "If it wasn't for me he wouldn't be where he is today," he maintains.

"I basically raised myself," Mayweather says. "My grandmother did what she could. When she got mad at me I'd go to my mom's house. My life was ups and downs." His father says he knows how much pain his incarceration caused his son, but insists he did the best he could. "I sent him to live with his grandmother," he says. "It wasn't like I left him with strangers."

In the absence of his father, boxing became an outlet for Mayweather.[1] As the elder Mayweather served his time, his son – with speed and an uncanny ring sense – put all his energies into boxing and dropped out of high school. "I knew that I was going to have to try to take care of my mom and I made the decision that school wasn't that important at the time and I was going to have to box to earn a living," Mayweather says.

The Floyd Mayweather Jr. and his mummy

Amateur career

Mayweather had an amateur record of 84–8 and won national <u>Golden Gloves</u> championships in 1993 (at 106 <u>lb</u>), 1994 (at 114 lb), and 1996 (at 125 lb).[He was nicknamed "Pretty Boy" by his amateur teammates because he had relatively few scars, a result of the <u>defensive techniques</u> that his father and uncle (Roger Mayweather) had taught him. In his orthodox defensive stance Mayweather often utilizes the "shoulder roll," an old-school boxing technique in which the right hand is held normally (or slightly higher than normal), the left hand is down around the <u>midsection</u> and the lead <u>shoulder</u> is raised high on the <u>cheek</u> in order to cover the <u>chin</u> and block punches. The right hand (as in the <u>orthodox stance</u>) is used as it normally would be: to block punches coming from the other side, such as left <u>hooks</u>. From this stance Mayweather blocks, slips and deflects most of his opponents' punches (even when cornered) by twisting left and right to the rhythm of their punches.

Floyd-Mayweather-Girlfriend-Shantel-Jackson

Floyd Mayweather Jr.'s Ex Josie Harris

Floyd Mayweather 's four teenagers : Sons Koraun, 17, and Zion, 16, and daughters Iyanna, 17, and Jirah, 13

1996 Olympics

At the <u>1996 Olympics</u> in <u>Atlanta</u>, Mayweather won a <u>bronze medal</u> by reaching the semi-finals of the <u>featherweight</u> (57-<u>kg</u>) division.

In the opening round Mayweather led 10–1 on points over <u>Bakhtiyar Tileganov</u> of <u>Kazakhstan</u>, before winning when the fight was stopped. In the second round, Mayweather outpointed <u>Artur Gevorgyan</u> of <u>Armenia</u> 16–3. In the quarterfinals, the 19-year-old Mayweather narrowly defeated 22-year-old <u>Lorenzo Aragon</u> of <u>Cuba</u> in an all-action bout to win 12–11, becoming the first U.S boxer to defeat a Cuban in 20 years. The last time this occurred was the <u>1976 Summer Olympics</u>, when the U.S Olympic boxing team captured five gold medals; among the recipients was Sugar

Ray Leonard. In his semifinal bout against eventual silver medalist Serafim Todorov of Bulgaria, Mayweather lost by a controversial decision (similar to Roy Jones Jr.'s highly controversial decision loss to Park Si-hun at the 1988 Summer Olympics). Referee Hamad Hafaz Shouman of Egypt mistakenly raised Mayweather's hand (thinking he had won), while the decision was announced giving the bout to the Bulgarian.

The U.S. team filed a protest over the Mayweather bout, claiming the judges were intimidated by Bulgaria's Emil Jetchev (head of the boxing officials) into favoring the Bulgarian Todorov by a 10–9 decision in the 125-pound semifinal bout. Three of Jetchev's countrymen were in gold medal bouts. Judge Bill Waeckerle (one of the four U.S judges working the games for the International Amateur Boxing Federation) resigned as Olympic Games and federation judge after Mayweather lost the decision, which was loudly booed by the crowd at the Alexander Memorial Coliseum. "I refuse to be part of an organization that continues to conduct its officiating in this manner", Waeckerle wrote in his letter of resignation to federation president Anwar Chowdhry.

In the official protest U.S. team manager Gerald Smith said Mayweather landed punches that were not counted, while Todorov was awarded points without landing a punch. "The judging was totally incompetent," Waeckerle said. The judges failed to impose a mandatory two-point deduction against Todorov after he was warned five times by the referee for slapping. "Everybody knows Floyd Mayweather is the gold-medal favorite at 57 kilograms," Mayweather said afterward. "In America, it's known as 125 pounds. You know and I know I wasn't getting hit. They say he's the world champion. Now you all know who the real world champion is."

Featherweight Olympic qualification

- Defeated William Jenkins RSC/TKO-3
- Defeated James Baker RSCH/TKO-1
- Lost to Augie Sanchez PTS (11–12)
- Defeated Carlos Navarro PTS (31–11)
- Defeated Augie Sanchez PTS (12–8) in the box-offs
- Defeated Augie Sanchez PTS (20–10) in the box-offs

Olympic results

- Defeated Bakhtiyar Tileganov (Kazakhstan) RSCI/TKO-2
- Defeated Artur Gevorgyan (Armenia) PTS (16–3)
- Defeated Lorenzo Aragon (Cuba) PTS (12–11)
- Lost to Serafim Todorov (Bulgaria) PTS (9–10)*

Decision was protested unsuccessfully by the U.S. team

Professional career

Super featherweight

Mayweather fought his first professional bout on October 11, 1996 against fellow newcomer Roberto Apodaca, who was knocked out in round two. Mayweather's trainer at the time was his uncle, Roger Mayweather; his father was still imprisoned after his conviction for illegal drug trafficking in 1993. The latter took over as his son's trainer when he was released from prison (after Mayweather Jr.'s 14th fight—a second-round knockout of Sam Girard). From 1996 to early 1998, Mayweather won most of his fights by knockout or TKO.

Early in his pro-career, Mayweather received praise from all corners of the boxing world and was touted as a pugilistic prodigy. During his fight with Tony Duran the ESPN commentator remarked, "Emmanuel Steward was quoted as saying there have been very few who have been more talented than this kid. He will probably win two or three world championships; I think he will go on to be the best ever".[IBHOF trainer and commentator Gil Clancy commented before Mayweather's ninth professional fight (against Jesus Chavez), "I thought that Floyd Mayweather was the outstanding pro prospect in the entire Olympic games".

Mayweather vs. Hernandez

In 1998, within two years of entering professional boxing, Mayweather decisively won his first world title (the WBC super featherweight (130 lb) championship) with an eighth-round technical knockout of *The Ring* world #1-ranked super featherweight Genaro Hernández after his opponent's cornerman stopped the fight. It was Hernández' first defeat in that weight class; he said after the fight, "He defeated me, he is quick, smart and I always knew he had the speed. I give him respect. He is a true champ".

With Mayweather's win he became lineal champion of the division; Genaro Hernández had previously beaten Azumah Nelson, whose dominance of the super-featherweight division had prompted boxing publications to give him the vacant lineal championship. *The Ring* stopped awarding belts to world champions in the 1990s, but began again in 2002. Nelson won his lineal status during the 1990s; therefore, *The Ring's* vacant title was awarded neither to him, Hernández, nor Mayweather (although Mayweather was *The Ring's* #1-ranked super featherweight).

Mayweather became the first 1996 U.S. Olympian to win a world title. Following his victory Mayweather's promoter Bob Arum said, "We believe in our heart of hearts that Floyd Mayweather is the successor in a line that starts with Ray Robinson, goes to Muhammad Ali, then Sugar Ray Leonard...We believe that he epitomizes that style of fighting". After capturing the title Mayweather defended it against contender Angel Manfredy with a TKO in round two, giving Manfredy his first defeat in four years.

By the end of 1998 Mayweather was ranked by *The Ring* as the #8-ranked pound-for-pound best boxer in the world, and became one of the youngest recipients of *The Ring's* Fighter of the Year award (21, the same age Sugar Ray Robinson and Muhammad Ali were when winning their first awards). In 1999, Mayweather continued his domination of the super featherweight division by defending his title three more times. The second defense of his title was against the Argentine Carlos Rios, which he won in a unanimous decision. Mayweather, fighting past the eighth round for only the third time in his career, won on the judges' scoring 120–110, 119–108, and 120–109.

Mayweather's third title defense was against Justin Juuko, which he won via knockout in the ninth round. Juuko could not beat the count of 10 by referee Mitch Halpern, and the fight ended in Mayweather's favor 80 seconds into that (the ninth) round.[1] His final title defense in 1999 was against Carlos Gerena, with Mayweather winning in a seventh-round referee technical decision (RTD). Mayweather said after the fight, "I want to show the world that along with Oscar De La Hoya and Roy Jones Jr., I'm the best fighter in the world". This dominance did not go unnoticed in the boxing world; by the end of the year, the 22-year-old Mayweather was ranked *The Ring's* #2 pound-for-pound best boxer in the world (behind Roy Jones Jr.)

Before making the fifth successful defense of his title against former WBC Featherweight Champion Gregorio Vargas in early 2000, Mayweather fired his father as his manager and replaced him with James Prince. A few months after the fight, the rift between father and son grew when Mayweather also fired the elder Mayweather as his trainer. In a 2004 interview Mayweather said that although he loves his father, he had a better chemistry with Roger because his father had put too much pressure on him to be perfect. Mayweather, in his fifth title defense, won a near-shutout over "Goyo" Vargas in Las Vegas. During the 10th round, when Mayweather overheard HBO announcer Jim Lampley say that the champ had switched to a southpaw stance for the second time in the bout he leaned ringside and said "It was the third time". After a six-month layoff, Mayweather was still elusive. During the sixth round, Mayweather dropped Vargas with a hook to the ribs and cruised to a unanimous decision.

Roger Mayweather returned to his role as his nephew's trainer for his next bout; a non-title lightweight fight against Emanuel Burton, which Mayweather won in a ninth-round technical knockout.

Mayweather vs. Corrales

In one of the more definitive and memorable fights of his career Mayweather fought the hard-hitting, former IBF super-featherweight champion Diego Corrales (33–0, with 27 KOs). Coming into the bout Mayweather and Corrales were undefeated, and neither fighter had touched the canvas. Mayweather was *The Ring's* #2-ranked super featherweight in the world (and #7 pound-for-pound), while Corrales was the #1-ranked super featherweight in the world and #5 pound-for-pound. Before the fight was announced Mayweather had stated he wanted to fight Corrales, who was facing jail time for allegedly beating his pregnant wife. "I want Diego because I'm doing it for all the battered women across America", Mayweather said. "Just like he beat that woman, I'm going to beat him".

While both fighters were the same age (23), Corrales had several physical advantages over Mayweather: two inches in height, an inch in reach and (despite both arriving at the official weight-in at the 130-lb super-featherweight limit) unofficially 146 lbs, versus Mayweather's 136½ lbs.[1] In the bout, Mayweather won every round and knocked down Corrales five times (three times in round 7 and twice in round 10). After the fifth knockdown, Corrales' cornermen climbed onto the apron and stopped the fight, thereby establishing Mayweather as a claimant to boxing's mythical pound-for-pound title. At the time of the stoppage Mayweather was ahead on the scorecards, leading by 89–79, 90–79, and 90–78.[1] Throughout the fight, HBO commentators analyzed Mayweather. Larry Merchant stated, "Mayweather fights in a tradition of boxing and quick handedness that goes back in Michigan, all the way to fighters like Sugar Ray Robinson". Harold Lederman remarked,

Jim (Lampley), I gotta tell ya, I'm terribly impressed, I don't think I've seen an exhibition of boxing like this since Willie Pep, this kid is unbelievable, great legs, great speed, unbelievable ring-generalship. I mean he's got tremendous presence in that ring, Floyd Mayweather knows where he is, every minute of this fight...

Corrales landed 60 of 205 punches, and landed no more than nine punches in a single round. Mayweather landed 220 of 414 punches.[1] Corrales was unable to land any clean shots, as he stalked Mayweather through the early rounds. He landed an average of six punches a round, according to Compubox stats – the only time that a fighter has registered single digits in the 20 years CompuBox has been tracking punch statistics.[1]

After the fight Mayweather remarked, "I would like to fight Prince Naseem (Hamed), hopefully we can meet at 128 (Lbs) or he can come up to 130 (Lbs), we can fight or I can fight the winner of Casamayor..." "Prince Naseem isn't going to fight you," intervened HBO commentator Larry Merchant; who then chuckled and added: "after he saw this, it ain't gonna happen". "I really want to fight Prince Naseem..." Mayweather continued, "but hopefully I can face the winner of Casamayor (vs.) Freitas". Although neither fight materialised, Mayweather's opponent Diego Corrales would later hand Freitas (the winner of the Casamayor vs. Freitas fight) his first professional defeat and defeat Casamayor via controversial decision in a rematch of their first bout. Afterwards, Bob Arum was ecstatic about his new star. "Better than Sugar Ray Leonard", he asserted. "And did you see him at those press conferences...?"[1]

The fight was met with acclaim in the boxing world and sports in general. CBS said, "Floyd Mayweather Jr.'s speed was dazzling. His power was unexpected" and the BBC reported on "... a near flawless performance...". The *New York Daily News* reported that "Floyd Mayweather Jr., displaying blazing speed and punishing power..."[1] and *Sports Illustrated* reported "... a fistic masterpiece".[1]

On October 10, 2001, boxing trainer Eddie Futch died at age 90. Tim Smith of the New York *Daily News* remembered an encounter with the trainer in an article.

One of the last times I saw Futch was before the Floyd Mayweather Jr.-Diego Corrales junior lightweight title bout in Vegas. Futch was talking about how much he admired Mayweather's style, how Mayweather was such a beautiful boxer, able to slip along the ropes and avoid punches. Corrales said he was going to neutralize Mayweather's hand speed by hitting Mayweather on the arms. 'I guess he thinks he's going to stand there and let him hit him on the arms all night,' said Futch, who correctly predicted that Mayweather would completely dismantle Corrales in a defensive masterpiece. Futch had a way of cutting to the heart of a matter. I don't know anyone in boxing who won't miss him. I don't know anyone in boxing that can take his place.

On May 26, 2001 Floyd Mayweather, fighting in his hometown of Grand Rapids, pounded out a 12-round unanimous decision over future IBF super featherweight titleholder Carlos Hernández to retain his WBC super-featherweight title. Calling it "one of the toughest nights of my career", the 130-pound champion overcame injuries in both hands to improve his record to 26–0. "He is a very, very tough fighter", Mayweather said of the challenger, whose record fell to 33–3–1. "I'm disappointed in my performance." Mayweather suffered the first knockdown of his career when he hit Hernández with a left hook in round six, which caused him sufficient pain that he dropped his injured left hand to the canvas. He wasn't hit, but was given a standing eight-count by the referee.

Mayweather's last fight in the super-featherweight division was against future super featherweight and lightweight titleholder Jesús Chávez. Chávez was the WBC's top-ranked contender and came into the fight with a 31-bout winning streak. This was Mayweather's eighth defense of the WBC super-featherweight title, which he had held for more than three years. He won when Chávez's corner stopped the fight after round nine. Mayweather had such difficulty making weight for this fight that he did not eat for four days before the weigh-in. Chávez stated after the fight, "He's [Mayweather] the champ! And now I become his number-one fan".

Mayweather commented after the fight, "Although it will take some time to make the match, I want to fight Kostya Tszyu".Tszyu, an Australian-based Russian, by then had established himself as the best light welterweight in the world. Mayweather did not get a chance to fight Tszyu, but went on to fight Ricky Hatton (who defeated Tszyu and won his *Ring* light welterweight championship). By the end of 2001, Mayweather was still ranked *The Ring* #1 super featherweight and #5 best pound-for-pound boxer in the world.

Lightweight

Mayweather vs. Castillo I

In his first fight as a lightweight, Mayweather took on World Boxing Council (WBC) champion and *The Ring* #1-ranked lightweight José Luis Castillo. Despite both fighters officially meeting the 135-lb lightweight limit, Mayweather came to the ring weighing unofficially 138½ lbs to Castillo's 147½ lbs. He defeated Castillo, winning the WBC and vacant *The Ring* and lineal lightweight titles with a 12-round unanimous decision at the MGM Grand Garden Arena before a crowd of 6,920. With Mayweather's win, he became the first lineal lightweight champion since Pernell Whitaker. Judges Jerry Roth and John Keane scored it 115–111 and judge Anek Hongtongkam scored it 116–111, a decision that was loudly booed by the pro-Castillo crowd. The Associated Press had Mayweather winning, 115–111; the New York *Daily News* scorecard also had Mayweather winning, 116–112.

Castillo (45–5–1, 41 KOs) could not touch Mayweather in the first round, with Castillo throwing 27 punches and landing only three. After round one Larry Merchant pointed out, "Mayweather made a comment in the corner about his left shoulder. We'll see if something's wrong with it, he seems to be rotating it, trying to keep it loose". George Foreman noted likewise, adding "'Massage my left shoulder', he (Mayweather) said, that's not a good sign".

In the first minute of the second round Castillo went down on a shot by Mayweather, which was ruled a slip by the referee. Later in the fight Harold Lederman alluded to it, saying "By the way, that knockdown in the second round [is] extremely questionable, I thought Floyd did throw a left hook and this guy [Castillo] went down at the end of the hook but what you going to do, it's a judgement call by the referee, so it doesn't go as a 10–8 round..." Drakulich took a point from Castillo for hitting on the break in the eighth round after several warnings throughout the fight. With Castillo repeatedly hitting on the break, this led to a large number of his punches landing. George Foreman agreed with the decision ("That's what you want a referee to do"), although his counterpart Larry Merchant had an alternative view: "I think this referee has been altogether too involved in the fight. Too officious".[1] Drakulich struck again in the ninth round, this time taking a point away from Mayweather for using his elbows. Mayweather won the fight by using his jab effectively and staying away from Castillo for much of the fight. Having injured his left shoulder on the last day of training, he changed to a southpaw stance on several occasions to throw more right-handed punches.

At the end of the fight, Harold Lederman had Castillo winning 115–111. ESPN's Max Kellerman disputed Lederman's scoring, writing in his boxing column: "Harold Lederman, the (HBO) unofficial ringside television judge, gave the third round to Castillo, which I think demonstrates that Mayweather suffers from the same scoring syndrome that afflicted Pernell Whitaker. Mayweather is so seldom hit cleanly in his face, that when a clean shot is landed against him it registers all out of proportion in the observer's mind. Meanwhile, the three clean shots Mayweather just landed against his opponent do not make the same kind of impression".

Compubox statistics indicated that Castillo landed more overall punches and significantly more power shots over the course of the fight; however, these statistics did not accurately reflect the judging (rounds are scored in isolation). Mayweather also outscored Castillo in jabs thrown and landed. Lederman's scoring for this fight may be seen as inconsistent; in both Bernard Hopkins vs. Jermain Taylor fights Lederman had Taylor winning 115–113, despite Hopkins landing more overall punches and significantly more power shots during both fights. Taylor threw and landed more jabs, however.

In the post-fight interview Mayweather said, "My last training day, I hurt my rotator cuff in my left shoulder, so I couldn't use my jab the way I want to. My left wasn't as strong as I wanted it to be, but I didn't want to have no excuses, you know, like other champions, you know, when they get hurt they won't even show up to the fight. I get hurt I keep fighting, you know, I want to bring the fans a victory".

Mayweather vs. Castillo II

Due to the closeness of their first bout, Mayweather accepted an immediate rematch with José Luis Castillo which took place on December 7, 2002. Before the rematch, Mayweather reiterated that he had torn his left rotator cuff two days before the first fight and could not throw a jab or a left hook. He had surgery following the controversial decision over Castillo, and said his shoulder had fully healed.

The smaller Mayweather was again outweighed by Castillo on the night of the fight; Castillo weighed 147 lbs, to Mayweather's 138. In the rematch Mayweather used his footwork, combinations and jab to earn another unanimous decision. There were no knockdowns or notable exchanges in the fight; the judgment was close, with Mayweather winning 115–113 on two scorecards and 116–113 on a third. The Associated Press had Mayweather winning 116–112;[HBO unofficial scorer Harold Lederman and fellow analyst Larry Merchant both scored it 115–113 for Mayweather.

On April 19, 2003 Mayweather defended his WBC lightweight title in a unanimous decision over Dominican Victoriano Sosa. Mayweather (30–0) fought a tactically-sound 12-round bout against an aggressive Sosa (35–3–2). His next fight (on November 1 of the same year) was in his hometown of Grand Rapids against WBC #1-ranked contender Phillip N'dou, whose record was 31–1 with 30 KOs. During the run-up to the fight Nelson Mandela invited N'dou to his office for a pep talk before his departure for the U.S., advising him to "keep Mayweather on the outside with the jab, work the body and the head will become available". South African president Thabo Mbeki, in a note, said he had "full confidence" N'dou would put on a performance to make all South Africans proud and would return home with the WBC belt. When told of his opponent's high-level support Mayweather responded, "Nelson Mandela's a great man, he's big in America, but Mandela can't get in there and fight for him".

In the fifth round, Mayweather connected with a series of straight rights and lefts; when N'dou would not go down, Mayweather gave a little smile and continued the barrage. He dominated his opponent, before flooring him with a series of rights in the seventh round. N'dou got up on shaky legs, forcing a stoppage at 1:50. At times during the fight, Mayweather (in black trunks outlined with fur) seemed to toy with N'dou.[1] By the end of 2003, Mayweather was still *The Ring's* lightweight champion and the #5-ranked best pound-for-pound boxer in the world

Light welterweight

Mayweather vs. Corley

Mayweather, at 27, made his 140-pound debut by defeating former titlist DeMarcus "Chop Chop" Corley, knocking him down twice officially in rounds eight and ten and scoring a decision of 119–108 (twice) and 119–107. The fight was billed as a WBC elimination bout, with the winner earning a shot at 140-pound champion Arturo Gatti. "Mayweather can flat-out fight", Corley's trainer Don Turner said. "He's like magic. He makes you move into the punches."[1] Shortly after this fight Mayweather would reach #1 on the *USA Today* pound-for-pound rankings, with middleweight champion Bernard Hopkins at #2.

Mayweather vs. Bruseles

On January 22, 2005 Mayweather fought Henry Bruseles in another WBC elimination bout, outclassing Bruseles throughout the first seven rounds. In round eight, Mayweather knocked Bruseles down twice and the fight was stopped. Mayweather's victory made him the mandatory challenger for Gatti's WBC light welterweight championship.

Mayweather vs. Gatti

The pay-per-view fight between Mayweather and *The Ring* #1-ranked contender Arturo Gatti took place June 25, 2005 in Atlantic City, New Jersey, where fans heavily supported Gatti. Before the fight Mayweather was confident, describing Gatti as "a C+ fighter," "a fake" and "a blown-up club fighter".[92] Mayweather entered the ring being carried on a chariot to the song "Another One Bites the Dust". Gatti entered the ring accompanied by the song "Thunderstruck" and was momentarily frightened by the pyrotechnics exploding. Near the end of round one, Mayweather pushed Gatti's head down in close; Gatti broke, leaving himself vulnerable while Mayweather continued landing punches. Gatti turned to the referee to complain; Mayweather capitalised, sending Gatti to the canvas with more shots for what was scored a knockdown.

Throughout the next five rounds, the quicker Mayweather landed nearly every shot against Gatti, who had no offense with which to return fire. Gatti's corner stopped the fight after round six, giving Mayweather his third world title.

In the post-fight interview Mayweather praised Gatti, claiming that his pre-fight comments "were just to sell tickets". To many boxing experts, Mayweather's dominance of Gatti solidified his position as one of the best pound-for-pound fighters in the world. Compubox had Mayweather out-landing Gatti 168–41, with Gatti landing only 10 power punches (anything other than a jab). Mayweather's fight with Gatti would be his last in the light-welterweight division; he would leave as *The Ring* #1-ranked contender, with Ricky Hatton as light-welterweight champion.

Welterweight

After his fight with Gatti, Mayweather moved up to the welterweight division. On November 19, 2005, Mayweather fought a non-title bout at 147 lb (67 kg) against welterweight Sharmba Mitchell. In round three, Mayweather knocked Mitchell down with a straight right hand to the head. In round six another straight right hand—this one to Mitchell's body—dropped Mitchell again, ending the fight.

Mayweather vs. Judah

On April 8, 2006, Mayweather defeated Zab Judah for the IBF welterweight title in a unanimous decision. Plans for the fight had been jeopardized after Judah lost the WBA, WBC and *The Ring* Welterweight titles to Carlos Baldomir on January 7, 2006; however, Mayweather's and Judah's camps reworked the contract and decided that the fight would go on. During the bout, Mayweather stayed calm during Judah's aggressive early rounds. He began to dominate Judah in round five, and the latter eventually bled. Late in the tenth round Judah hit Mayweather with a left hand that was clearly below the belt, following with a right-handed rabbit punch. Referee Richard Steele called time out with five seconds remaining in the round. Roger Mayweather entered the ring and approached Judah, but Steele restrained him; Judah's father (and trainer), Yoel Judah, entered the ring as well. Mayweather remained in the neutral corner while the Judahs scuffled with Roger (and others who had entered the ring), until police and security restored order. Roger was ejected, and the fight continued for the scheduled 12 rounds. Mayweather won by official scores of 116–112, 117–111, and 119–109. Compubox statistics showed him landing 188 punches, compared with 82 for Judah.

Five days after the fight, the Nevada State Athletic Commission (NSAC) decided not to overturn the result of the bout; however, Roger Mayweather was fined $200,000 and suspended for one year. The suspension stipulated that Roger could train Mayweather in the gym, but could not work the corner during fights. On April 17, 2006, the IBF ordered a rematch between Mayweather and Judah; however, the NSAC suspended Judah for one year on May 8 and Mayweather vacated the IBF title on June 20.

After his fight with Judah it was reported that Mayweather rejected an $8 million offer to fight Antonio Margarito, citing his split with promoter Bob Arum as the reason. However, Oscar De la Hoya postponed his decision until 2007, leaving Mayweather to obtain Mayweather Promotions and choose his next opponent. Mayweather considered moving up in weight again to fight light middleweight champion Cory Spinks, but because of negative publicity and Spinks' impending mandatory defense of his title, he decided to face WBC and *The Ring* welterweight champion Carlos Baldomir on November 4, 2006 in Las Vegas.[1]

Mayweather vs. Baldomir

Despite having not lost in over eight years, Baldomir was an underdog in the fight. Mayweather defeated him for both titles in a unanimous decision. Ringside punch statistics showed Mayweather landing 199 of 458 punches, while Baldomir landed 79 of 670. Mayweather earned $8 million for the fight; Baldomir was paid $1.6 million, career earnings highs for each fighter at the time.

During the fight Baldomir chased Mayweather, unable to land any meaningful shots but trying to be the busier fighter; Mayweather picked away with sharp jabs and hooks, cutting Baldomir over his left eye in the first round. This pattern continued throughout the fight; the defensive-minded Mayweather put on what many witnesses (and Mayweather himself) called a "boxing clinic" to take Baldomir's WBC, *The Ring* and lineal welterweight titles in a lopsided 12-round decision. Two judges had Mayweather winning all 12 rounds, with the third giving all but two rounds to Mayweather. After the fight, Mayweather proposed a match with Oscar De La Hoya.

With Mayweather's win, he became the first fighter since Roberto Durán to have captured *The Ring* titles in both the lightweight and welterweight divisions.[*citation needed*] He also captured his third lineal championship in as many weight classes (super featherweight, lightweight and welterweight), following in the footsteps of Henry Armstrong and Sugar Ray Leonard.

Light middleweight

Mayweather vs. De La Hoya

Mayweather's next match was the long-anticipated fight against six-division champion and WBC light-middleweight titleholder Oscar De La Hoya on May 5, 2007. De La Hoya's belt was on the line, which required Mayweather to move up in weight from 147 pounds to 154. However, Mayweather was outweighed by more than 10 pounds the night of the fight, coming in at only 150 pounds. Despite De La Hoya's insistence that money was not a factor, the Mayweather-De La Hoya bout set the record for most PPV buys for a boxing match with 2.7 million households, breaking the previous record of 1.95 million for Evander Holyfield-Mike Tyson II. About $120 million in revenue was generated by the PPV, another record. Including percentages De La Hoya earned $58 million for the bout, the highest purse ever for a fighter; the previous record was $35 million, held by Tyson and Holyfield. Mayweather earned about $25 million for the fight.[1]

At one time, Floyd Mayweather, Sr. negotiated to train Oscar De La Hoya and be in his corner during the fight, but De La Hoya decided to train with Freddie Roach. Mayweather won the fight by a split decision in 12 rounds, capturing the WBC title. However, many analysts and ringside observers felt Mayweather should have received a unanimous decision. During the early rounds De La Hoya had some success cutting off the ring, attempting to pound Mayweather on the inside. Despite his activity on the inside, however, many of De La Hoya's punches were ineffective and landed on Mayweather's arms or shoulders. By the middle of the fight, it was seen as an even bout by the announcers. Mayweather turned the tide in the middle and late rounds, often hitting De La Hoya at will. Official scorecards read 116–112 (Mayweather), 115–113 (Mayweather), and 115–113 (De La Hoya). Compubox had Mayweather out-landing De La Hoya 207–122 in total punches and 134–82 in power punches, with better accuracy throughout the fight. After the bout Mayweather contemplated retirement, saying he had nothing left to prove in the boxing world.

Return to welterweight and retirement

Mayweather vs. Hatton

After his fight with De La Hoya, Mayweather decided to relinquish his WBC light-middleweight championship,[1] retaining his welterweight title. On July 28, 2007, it was announced that Mayweather would come out of his brief retirement to fight *The Ring* light welterweight champion Ricky Hatton; the bout was promoted by De La Hoya's promotion company (Golden Boy Promotions) and Mayweather's Mayweather Promotions. The fight was entitled "Undefeated"; it took place December 8, 2007 at the MGM Grand Garden Arena, Las Vegas, Nevada, the biggest welterweight showdown between two undefeated fighters since De La Hoya met Félix Trinidad in 1999. During the run-up to their fight Mayweather claimed he was the greatest boxer ever: "I respect what Robinson and Ali did for the sport. But I am the greatest and this is my time."

Mayweather controlled the fight from the beginning, knocking Hatton out in the 10th round to retain the welterweight championship. Hatton suffered a cut over his right eye in round three; from that point, his pace and movement began to slow. In round six, Hatton lost a point for punching the back of Mayweather's head as he was draped over the ropes. During the tenth round, Hatton was caught by a checked left hook thrown from Mayweather's hip; after falling headfirst into the turnbuckle, he hit the floor. Hatton made it to his feet, but was dazed. Two more lefts in quick succession knocked Hatton down again, and referee Cortez stopped the fight at 1:35 of round ten. Official scorecards read 88–82, 89–81, and 89–81 at the time of stoppage, all in favor of Mayweather.

After the fight, Mayweather said that Hatton was one of his toughest, most tenacious opponents. Mayweather announced his retirement from boxing to concentrate on his promotional company, saying he wanted Hatton to be his first client.

COMBACK

Mayweather vs. Marquez
On May 2, 2009, it was confirmed that Mayweather was coming out of a 21-month retirement to fight *The Ring* lightweight champion and #2 pound-for-pound Juan Manuel Márquez, at a catch weight of 144 lb on July 18 at the MGM Grand in Las Vegas on HBO PPV.[112] The fight was postponed due to a rib

Mayweather during his comeback bout against Juan Manuel Márquez, 2009

The fight took place on September 19 in conjunction with Mexican Independence Day, traditionally a big boxing weekend. During the official weigh-in for their 142 lb bout, Mayweather failed to meet the weight limit at 146 lb and was fined as a result. However, it was later revealed that the contract was changed so that Mayweather could make weight within the welterweight limit of 140–147 lb as long as Marquez received a large guarantee. Mayweather won a unanimous decision after 12 rounds in a lopsided fight; scorecards read 120–107, 119–108, and 118–109. Marquez landed 12 percent of his total 583 punches, while Mayweather landed 59 percent of his 490 total punches. This fight marked only the fifth time in boxing history that a non-heavyweight fight sold more than 1 million pay-per-view households, with HBO generating a revenue of approximately $52 million. Four of the other fights featured Oscar De La Hoya as the main event, making this fight the one of two events where a non-heavyweight fight sold over 1 million PPVs without Oscar De La Hoya. The other fight was Manny Pacquiao versus Miguel Cotto, which sold 1.25 million PPVs.

Mayweather vs. Mosley

Negotiations for a proposed match between Mayweather and *The Ring* #3 pound-for-pound Shane Mosley began right after Andre Berto pulled out of his scheduled January 30 unification bout with Mosley due to the 2010 Haiti earthquake. Both sides eventually agreed to fight on May 1, 2010, for Mosley's WBA super-welterweight title. It was later revealed that Mayweather refused to pay sanctioning fees required by the WBA, saying "All belts do is collect dust". However, the belt was only on the line for Mosley to defend against Mayweather. Both Mayweather and Mosley agreed to Olympic-style testing for this bout.

Mosley started the fight well, landing two solid right hands in round two which caused Mayweather's knees to buckle. Mayweather recovered well and went on to dominate the remainder of the fight, out-boxing Mosley and showing more aggression than in his previous recent fights. Mayweather eventually won a unanimous decision, with the judges scoring the fight 119–109, 119–109, and 118–110. In round four Compubox found Mosley throwing seven power punches without taking any, making Mayweather the second boxer (after Roy Jones Jr.) to go an entire round without being hit by a power punch. After the fight, president of Golden Boy Promotions Oscar De La Hoya stated that he believed Mayweather was the best in the game.

The fight was the second-bestselling non-heavyweight pay-per-view bout in boxing history, with 1.4 million purchases. HBO reported that the fight generated $78.3 million in revenue. After the bout Mayweather expressed interest in moving up in weight to capture a world title in six different weight classes, and to challenge newly crowned middleweight champion Sergio Martinez.[122]

Negotiations with Manny Pacquiao

On December 5, 2009, ESPN reported that eight-division world champion Manny Pacquiao signed a contract to fight Mayweather on March 13,

2010. Shortly afterward, Pacquiao denied ever signing a contract to fight Mayweather, telling *FanHouse*, "There are still some things that need to be negotiated."[1]

According to *Yahoo! Sports*, an eight-page contract was sent on December 11, 2009, by Golden Boy Promotions on behalf of Mayweather to Top Rank, representing Pacquiao, that proposed a 50–50 financial split between the sides for a fight to take place on March 13, 2010.

The eight-page agreement was so detailed that it indicated which of the two fighters would step onto the scale first at the weigh-in (Pacquiao), who would walk to the ring first (Pacquiao), who would be introduced first (Mayweather) and who had first choice of the locker room (Mayweather). It detailed that the bout would have been on HBO Pay-Per-View at a cost of $59.95. Billing was to be "Mayweather vs. Pacquiao, presented by Top Rank, Golden Boy Promotions, Mayweather Promotions and M-P Promotions in association with [approved sponsors and the site]." The contract also called for both fighters to submit to Olympic-style drug testing.

A Mayweather-Pacquiao bout at that time was expected to be the largest-grossing fight in history, in which total revenues could reach $300 million. Experts predicted the fight would sell between 2.5 million and 3 million pay-per-views in the U.S.

In a video titled "Boxing Legend Freddie Roach Updates Us On Pacquiao" uploaded to YouTube on December 11, 2009, Pacquiao's trainer, Freddie Roach, revealed the first hint about Mayweather's request for Olympic-style drug testing, telling roving reporter Elie Seckbach, "I hear negotiations are a little shady. Schaefer and them are unhappy about something. They want Olympic-style drug testing. I said, 'Yeah, no problem.' I said, 'Whatever you want.' Since we accepted that, now they're running scared again."

On December 13, 2009, Pacquiao's adviser, Michael Koncz, said Mayweather's request for Olympic-style drug testing was a laughing matter and they had no concerns whatsoever about it. "Our reaction is, 'So what?' We know Manny doesn't take any illegal drugs or anything. And none of this is getting under Manny's skin or anything. I'm here with Manny, and to him, it's like a joke. It's a laughing matter," said Koncz.

After reports had surfaced that both parties had agreed to all terms, Golden Boy Promotions released a press release on December 22, 2009, revealing that Pacquiao was unwilling to comply with the Olympic-style drug testing requested by Team Mayweather. The following day, Bob Arum, Top Rank founder and CEO, declared the fight was off and Pacquiao would be facing a different opponent:

We appeased Mayweather by agreeing to a urine analysis at any time, and blood testing before the press conference and after the fight. Mayweather pressed for blood testing even up to the weigh-in. He knew that Manny gets freaked out when his blood gets taken and feels that it weakens him. This is just harassment and, to me, just signaled that he didn't want the fight.

Arum told David Mayo of the *Grand Rapids Press*. Not long after declaring that the fight was off, Arum had a change of heart and offered Mayweather a 24-hour take-it-or-leave-it deadline to accept Team Pacquiao's terms for drug testing. Top Rank sent out a press release explaining their position on Mayweather's request for random Olympic-style drug testing. In it, Arum said Pacquiao was willing to submit to as many random urine tests requested, but as far as random blood tests were concerned, he was only willing to subject himself to 3 tests—one in January, one 30 days from the bout (no later than February 13) and one immediately after the fight:

Let's be very clear on the real issues we differ on. It's not about being tested....It's about who does the testing and the scheduling of the procedures....The major issue related to the testing rests with which independent agency will administer these tests. The United States Anti-Doping Agency (USADA) cannot do it because they will not amend its procedures to accommodate the blood testing schedule we have outlined. USADA, under its guidelines, would have the right to administer random blood tests as many times as they want up to weigh-in day and that is ludicrous.

Freddie Roach told Lance Pugmire of the *Los Angeles Times* on December 22 that he would prefer for Pacquiao to give his final blood sample a week before the bout and no later than 72 hours before.

On December 28, 2009, video from an episode of HBO's *Pacquiao-Hatton: 24/7* surfaced on the internet showing Pacquiao giving blood in the weeks leading up to his May 2, 2009, bout with Ricky Hatton. Documents confirmed that the video was recorded on April 8, 2009, 24 days prior to the fight and past the 30-day cut-off date that Pacquiao had demanded for a Mayweather fight.

Both sides agreed to enter into <u>mediation</u> on January 7, 2010, in hopes of coming to an agreement on the blood testing issue. Retired federal judge Daniel Weinstein, who successfully resolved a prior dispute between Top Rank and Golden Boy Promotions, would again act as mediator. Two days later, after hours of negotiating during mediation, Arum declared that the fight was officially off after Mayweather refused to agree to a 24-day cut-off date. Mayweather revealed that he offered a 14-day cut-off date to Team Pacquiao, but it was rejected.

Mayweather Promotions CEO Leonard Ellerbe declared on January 18, 2010, that random blood and urine testing will be implemented in all of Mayweather's future fights, regardless of the opponent. On February 13, 2010, in an exclusive interview with David Mayo of The *Grand Rapids Press*, Mayweather said, "I gave him [Pacquiao] a chance, up to 14 days out. But my new terms are all the way up to the fight. They can come get us whenever, all the way up to the fight, random drug test. That's what it is."

After the failed negotiations, both fighters moved on to instead face other opponents. On March 13, 2010, Pacquiao defeated <u>Joshua Clottey</u> via unanimous decision, and on May 1, 2010, Mayweather beat Shane Mosley by a unanimous decision.

Pacquiao was quoted by the *Manila Bulletin* on May 20, 2010, as saying, "As long as they're not getting a large amount of blood, I am willing to give out blood as close to two weeks before the fight." On the same day, Mayweather revealed that he would be taking the rest of 2010, and possibly 2011, off.

On June 10, 2010, Oscar De La Hoya said negotiations for a Mayweather-Pacquiao fight were close to being finalized. Speaking to Spanish-language sport show *República Deportiva*, De La Hoya briefly talked about the current status of negotiations and, with a grin on his face, said that the two sides were extremely close to making the biggest fight in boxing a reality. "These negotiations have been real difficult for various reasons, but we're really close to finalizing the contracts, even though they've been complicated," he commented. "Today, I can't really talk about the negotiations, but we're really close." A week later, Golden Boy Promotions CEO Richard Schaefer refuted De La Hoya's comments. "I saw those quotes as well, and I had no idea what Oscar was talking about. And I called him up and asked him about them, and he said that he was misquoted," Schaefer explained to Lem Satterfield of *FanHouse*.

Arum declared on June 30, 2010, that there were no longer any issues and the decision was up to Mayweather. "That's all been resolved," Arum stated to Kevin Iole of *Yahoo! Sports* regarding the dispute over random blood and urine drug testing. Arum would also tell the *Las Vegas Review-Journal*, "There's no longer any issues....The question is whether Mayweather is willing to fight this year." He would reiterate that comment to the *Manila Bulletin*, stating, "It's now up to Mayweather if he wants to fight."

On July 13, 2010, Arum issued a July 16 midnight deadline for Mayweather. "Mayweather has until the end of the week. He could wait until the last minute. If it's Friday [July 16] and it's 11 p.m., and he says we have a deal, we have a deal," Arum would explain to Dan Rafael of ESPN. On July 15, 2010, Top Rank's website unveiled an official countdown to the deadline entitled "Money" Time: Mayweather's Decision.

As soon as the deadline for Mayweather's response expired, Arum held a conference call. Arum revealed to the media that the negotiations he had been referring to consisted of a series of conversations with HBO Sports President Ross Greenburg. He also revealed that there was no actual direct communication with any representative from Team Mayweather or Golden Boy Promotions:

I had a couple of conversations with Ross [Greenburg] and I laid out all the terms that would be acceptable to our side and I also informed him about the concession that Manny had made regarding drug testing. He got back to me in a couple of weeks and told me that he had had discussions with Al Haymon, representing Floyd Mayweather, and that everything looked good and we were nearing a resolution...The subsequent conversations with Ross detailed to me conversations he had with Al Haymon. Nowhere was the name Richard Schaefer or Golden Boy mentioned, although I read, as you all did, Oscar's statement that a deal was close, so I assumed from that Haymon was keeping Schaefer and Golden Boy abreast of the situation.

During a Q & A session following his opening statement, Arum further explained, "We have never talked to anybody on the Mayweather side and all conversations on our part were through Ross Greenburg and he reported on all conversations on the Mayweather side from Al Haymon."

On July 19, 2010, Ellerbe denied that negotiations ever took place and nothing was ever agreed on. Ellerbe stated:

Here are the facts: Al Haymon, Richard Schaefer and myself speak to each other on a regular basis and the truth is no negotiations have ever taken place nor was there ever a deal agreed upon by Team Mayweather or Floyd Mayweather to fight Manny Pacquiao on November 13. Either Ross Greenburg or Bob Arum is not telling the truth, but history tells us who is lying.

Three days later, Schaefer backed Ellerbe's statement that negotiations never took place.

When asked via e-mail for his response to Ellerbe's denial that negotiations ever took place, Greenburg would respond to ESPN's Dan Rafael with the following reply: "As always we have no comment."

Regarding comments he made suggesting that contracts for the mega-fight were close to being finalized, De La Hoya told *BoxingScene.com* on July 26, 2010:

I think I said it because I get the question asked so many times that, obviously, I was fed up and tired of it and I just said like, yeah, yeah, it's gonna get made. So it was a quick answer that I should have obviously thought about. But, obviously, negotiations weren't going on. Nothing was going on.

Also on July 26, Greenburg released a statement saying that he had been negotiating with a representative from each side since May 2, 2010. "I had been negotiating with a representative from each side since May 2, carefully trying to put the fight together. Hopefully, someday this fight will happen. Sports fans deserve it," Greenburg revealed in a prepared statement sent out to select members of the media.

Schaefer again supported Ellerbe's denial of negotiations, and challenged both Greenburg and Arum to take lie detector tests. "I think it's unfortunate that Ross made that statement. I fully stand behind the statement I made. I have not negotiated with Ross and I am not aware of any negotiations that have taken place," Schaefer told ESPN.

On July 8, 2011, ESPN reported that Pacquiao was willing to agree to random drug testing—but not by the United States Anti-Doping Agency (USADA). "We have agreed in the Pacquiao camp to unlimited random testing done by a responsible, neutral organization," Arum told Yahoo.

We don't believe USADA is a neutral organization. I don't think anybody's test is as vigorous as the test administered by the Olympic Organization. And we can arrange for the Olympic Organization to handle the test under the supervision of the Athletic commission respective of the state where the fight is going to be held.

However, the following day, Pacquiao's top adviser, Michael Koncz, stated that Pacquiao had never agreed to testing until fight day. "Will we give blood five days, seven days before the fight? You know, that's something I have to talk to Manny about, but we have nothing to hide," Koncz said.

ESPN reported on January 20, 2012, that Mayweather called Pacquiao on the telephone and spoke directly with him in the Philippines. "He ask about a 50/50 split and I told him no that can't happen, but what can happen is you can make more money fighting me then [sic] you have made in your career," Mayweather said. Mayweather offered to pay him a flat fee of $40 million for a proposed fight but would not allow him to share in the revenue. Pacquiao said, "I spoke to Floyd...and he offered me an amount," Pacquiao said. "He didn't talk about the pay-per-views here and that's it. I can't agree with that. I told him I agree with 55 and 45 (split)."

Pacquiao appeared on the ESPN program *First Take* on September 20, 2012, and said he had no problem with the drug-testing issue. "No problem," Pacquiao said. "Whatever he wants to do." Pacquiao said he was willing to be tested even on the night of the fight. "No problem," he said. "Even the night of the fight. No problem."

On December 20, 2013, *The Daily Telegraph* reported that Mayweather said Pacquiao's association with promoter Bob Arum is the reason why the bout will not happen. "We all know the Pacquiao fight, at this particular time, will never happen, and the reason why the fight won't happen is because I will never do business with Bob Arum again in life, and Pacquiao is Bob Arum's fighter," Mayweather said.

Return to the ring

Mayweather vs. Ortiz

On June 7, 2011, Mayweather announced via Twitter that he was set to fight WBC welterweight champion and The Ring #2-ranked welterweight Victor Ortiz on September 17. Ortiz was Mayweather's first challenger in 16 months.[131] The fight took place at the MGM Grand Garden Arena. From round one, Mayweather used his speed, skills and accurate right hand to tag Ortiz repeatedly. Although Mayweather seemed in control through the first three rounds (judges' scores 30–27, 30–27, and 29–28 for Mayweather) in the fourth round Ortiz had some success, landing a few shots and stinging Mayweather before bulling him into the corner. He then rammed Mayweather in the face with an intentional headbutt, opening a cut on the inside and outside of Mayweather's mouth. Referee Joe Cortez immediately called time out and docked Ortiz a point for the blatant foul. Ortiz, apparently acknowledging his wrongdoing, hugged Mayweather in the corner and even appeared to kiss him.

Cortez motioned the fighters back together to resume the fight, without putting them in a neutral corner. Both fighters touched gloves, and Ortiz gave Mayweather another hug. At that moment, Cortez was not looking at the fighters. As Ortiz let go, Mayweather took advantage of Ortiz not having his hands up and unloaded a left hook which wobbled Ortiz. Ortiz then looked at the referee, and Mayweather connected with a flush right hand to Ortiz's face. Ortiz fell to the canvas, and was unable to beat Cortez's count as the crowd of 14,687 jeered Mayweather. After the fight Ortiz claimed that he was merely obeying the referee's instructions when he was "blindsided" by Mayweather, who defended his actions by saying that "In the ring, you have to protect yourself at all times".

Mayweather vs. Ortiz was purchased by 1.25 million homes with a value of $78,440,000 in pay-per-view revenue. These numbers make the event the second-highest-grossing non-heavyweight pay-per-view event of all time. Mayweather has appeared in the three biggest non-heavyweight pay-per-view events in the sport's history: Mayweather vs. Oscar De La Hoya ($136,853,700), Mayweather vs. Ortiz ($78,440,000), and Mayweather vs. Shane Mosley ($78,330,000).

Return to light middleweight

Mayweather vs. Cotto

Mayweather's adviser, Leonard Ellerbe, announced on November 2, 2011, that Mayweather would return to the ring on May 5, 2012, at the MGM Grand Garden Arena in Las Vegas. After negotiations with Manny Pacquiao failed again, on February 1, 2012, it was confirmed that Mayweather would be moving up in weight to fight WBA super welterweight champion and *The Ring* #1-ranked light middleweight Miguel Cotto. The WBC put their super welterweight diamond belt at stake.

On the evening of Saturday, May 5, Mayweather defeated Cotto in 12 rounds by a unanimous decision, improving his record to 43–0. Mayweather used movement and outboxed Cotto in the middle of the ring for the first few rounds. Beginning in rounds three and four Cotto cut the ring off from Mayweather, forcing the latter to fight from the ropes. However, Mayweather seemed to outfight Cotto from the ropes with his combinations and by rolling with most of Cotto's punches. Cotto had more success in the middle rounds, landing his jab and body shots on Mayweather and effectively trapping him on the ropes. The later rounds were controlled by Mayweather, who boxed more in the center of the ring late in the fight. In the 12th round Mayweather's uppercut stunned and hurt Cotto, but Cotto was able to fight until the end. The judges scored the fight a unanimous decision for Mayweather by scores of 118–110, 117–111, and 117–111. After the fight, Mayweather said Cotto was the toughest fighter he ever faced.

CompuBox had Mayweather outlanding and outworking Cotto in the fight by a significant margin. Mayweather landed 26 percent of his total punches (179 out of 687), compared with 21 percent (105 out of 506) for Cotto. In power punches, Mayweather landed 128 of 382 (34 percent), compared with 75 of 329 (23 percent) for Cotto.[1] Mayweather earned the biggest guaranteed purse in boxing history ($32 million) when he fought Cotto, according to contracts filed with the Nevada State Athletic Commission. The Mayweather-Cotto fight generated $94 million in PPV revenue from 1.5 million purchases, making it the second-biggest non-heavyweight fight in history (after Mayweather's fight with Oscar De La Hoya).

Jail term and repercussions

On June 1, 2012, Mayweather reported to the Clark County Detention Center in Las Vegas to serve his 87-day jail term for domestic abuse. After serving two months, he was released from prison on August 3, 2012. On February 4, 2015, Mayweather, who was planning to do a tour in Australia, was denied a visa on the basis of his criminal record and jail term.

Mandatory title defense at welterweight

Mayweather vs. Guerrero

Mayweather returned to the ring on May 4, 2013, at the MGM Grand Garden Arena to face the WBC interim welterweight champion, *Ring* No. 3 ranked welterweight, and the WBC's mandatory challenger Robert Guerrero. This was Mayweather's first fight since being released from jail, and was the first time Mayweather has fought on Showtime PPV after a long relationship with HBO. Mayweather was guaranteed $32 million for the fight. The first couple rounds were fairly even, with Mayweather attempting to counter and time Guerrero, while Guerrero was attempting to drive Mayweather to the ropes and make it a rough fight. After the first couple rounds, Mayweather was in complete control, almost hitting Guerrero at will with right hand leads, counters, hooks, and effectively timing Guerrero the rest of the fight. Mayweather won the fight on all three scorecards 117–111. Although no official tallies are reported, according to Showtime Sports executive Stephen Espinoza, the fight had exceeded 1 million purchases in PPV.

Third return to light middleweight

Mayweather vs. Álvarez

Mayweather confirmed via Twitter that a deal was reached to face *Ring* No. 10 ranked pound for pound, WBC and WBA Super welterweight champion Saúl "Canelo" Álvarez in a championship bout on September 14, 2013, at the MGM Grand Garden Arena. A catchweight of 152 pounds was established for the fight.[Mayweather received a boxing record $41.5 million for the Alvarez fight, according to Leonard Ellerbe, Mayweather's confidant. The fight aired on pay-per-view and Mayweather won the match, with all scorecards in his favor except for one, which put Mayweather even with Alvarez.

Welterweight unification

Mayweather vs. Maidana I

Despite interest in a bout with Amir Khan, Mayweather announced that he would face Marcos Maidana on May 3, 2014, in a unification bout at MGM Grand Garden Arena, with Mayweather's WBC and *The Ring* welterweight titles at stake, as well as Maidana's WBA (Super) welterweight title. Mayweather won the bout via majority decision, with scores of 116–112, 117–111, and 114–114.[1]

Mayweather vs. Maidana II

A rematch with Maidana was later confirmed, with the bout taking place on September 13, 2014, at the MGM Grand Garden Arena, with Mayweather's WBA (Super), WBC and *The Ring* welterweight titles at stake, as well as Mayweather's WBC light middleweight title. Mayweather won the match via unanimous decision, with scores of 115–112, 116–111, and 116–111.

Mayweather vs. Pacquiao

Mayweather faced Manny Pacquiao, after negotiations spread over a number of years, on May 2, 2015, inside MGM Grand Garden Arena in Las Vegas. Mayweather dictated the pace early, controlling range with the jab. His deft movement and pivoting made Pacquiao, who landed only 19% of his punches, consistently miss. Mayweather was able to counter Pacquiao with his right hand constantly throughout the fight and won via unanimous decision with the scorecards reading 118–110, 116–112, and 116–112. The vast majority of media outlets (16/18) scored the bout in his favor. In the days following the fight, many casual observers felt the match failed to live up to expectations. Pacquiao told the media after the match that he was limited in the fight due to an injured right arm. *Sports Illustrated* reported that Pacquiao fought through a torn rotator cuff in his right shoulder, which will require surgery. Bob Arum revealed Pacquiao's injury to have been a persistent one dating back to 2008. Additionally Pacquiao's camp never requested a cortisone injection, which is allowed by the US Anti-Doping Agency, but rather a last minute toradol injection, which was declined by the Nevada State Athletic Commission. Mayweather, who originally had no plans on a rematch with Pacquiao, told ESPN's Stephen A. Smith in a text that he would be open to a rematch after Pacquiao recovers from shoulder surgery, however as of May 9, 2015, Mayweather stated "Did I text Stephen A. Smith and say I will fight him again? Yeah, but I change my mind. At this particular time, no, because he's a sore loser and he's a coward." On July 6, 2015, the World Boxing Organization (WBO) stripped Mayweather of his welterweight championship on technical grounds.

Second retirement

Mayweather vs. Berto

Mayweather confirmed through Instagram that he would defend the WBC, WBA (Super), and The Ring welterweight titles against WBA interim champion Andre Berto on September 12, 2015, at the MGM Grand Garden Arena.[165] Mayweather was able to pinpoint holes in Berto's guard and find a home for the jab early. He landed sharp counters and feint hooks while controlling range for the vast majority of the bout. Berto pushed the pace, but his aggressiveness fell short as Mayweather was highly mobile and closed the distance consistently. Mayweather hurt his left hand at the end of the ninth round but remained comfortable throughout the rest of the fight, winning via unanimous decision 117–111, 118–110, and 120–108. Keith Thurman noted, "Amazing speed ... he showed tremendous skill and talent." Mayweather announced his retirement in the ring after defeating Berto, walking away from the sport with an undefeated record of 49–0. The WBC declared his welterweight and super welterweight titles vacant in November 2015.

Second return

Mayweather vs. McGregor

The idea of a Mayweather comeback floated around April 2016 as rumors of Mayweather Promotions filing for trademarks of "TBE 50" and "TMT 50" hint that Mayweather may be targeting that 50th win. This was confirmed by posts from the U.S. Patent and Trademark website.

Around May 2016, another rumor started that a crossover fight between Mayweather and MMA star Conor McGregor is in the works. On May 7, 2016, Mayweather confirmed that he was the one who started the rumors regarding the potential clash. Mayweather followed it through with an Instagram post of an unofficial teaser poster showcasing both fighters. Mayweather reportedly talked to Freddie Roach to train McGregor for the fight in case it will happen. Dana White dismissed all the rumors and stated that Mayweather has yet to contact him in case he wants the fight to push through since McGregor is in contract with the UFC. On January 13, 2017, White continued his stance against a Mayweather and McGregor boxing matchup and insisted it will never happen due to McGregor's contract and even went as far as offering Mayweather to box McGregor in the UFC for $25 million.

On March 7, 2017, Mayweather urged McGregor to sign the contract hinting that a fight is really in the works. On March 10, 2017, Mayweather stated that only a fight with McGregor would make him come out of retirement. On March 16, 2017, Dana White backpedaled on his stance against Mayweather fighting McGregor and said that he would not deprive McGregor in making a massive payday. On May 18, 2017, McGregor reportedly agreed to all of Mayweather's updated terms and has signed the contract.

On June 14, 2017, after months of negotiations, both fighters announced via their Twitter accounts that they will fight on August 26, 2017 at the T-Mobile Arena in Las Vegas, Nevada. On August 24, 2017, it was. Announced that Mayweather and McGregor would be facing off for the WBC Money Belt.

WWE

Dealing With Bigshow

Mayweather appeared at WWE's No Way Out pay-per-view event on February 17, 2008 in Las Vegas, Nevada. He was involved in a storyline altercation with Big Show when Mayweather jumped a security barricade and attacked Big Show to help Rey Mysterio, whom Show had threatened to chokeslam. Mayweather originally assumed a babyface role in the story lines, which met with some resistance from fans. The attack resulted in Big Show receiving a broken nose. The following night on *Raw*, Big Show challenged Mayweather to a one-on-one No Disqualification match at WrestleMania XXIV, which Mayweather accepted. At WrestleMania, Mayweather defeated Big Show in a knockout with brass knuckles to maintain his unbeaten record. Mayweather was reportedly paid $20 million for the fight. 1 million PPV buys were reported for WrestleMania XXIV, grossing $23.8 million in revenue.

Mayweather was guest host for *Raw* in Las Vegas on August 24, 2009. He interfered with a tag-team match, which resulted in a loss for the Big Show (again a heel) and his partner Chris Jericho as Mayweather gave MVP brass knuckles to knock Jericho out, giving MVP and his new tag-team partner Mark Henry the win and a shot at the Unified WWE Tag Team Titles at WWE Breaking Point against Jeri-Show. He then celebrated with Henry and MVP, turning face. Later that night, he was involved in a backstage segment with Vince McMahon, D-Generation X, and Carlito, helping McMahon prepare for his six-man tag team match against The Legacy and DX. During the segment, McMahon knocked out Carlito.

Dancing with the Stars

Mayweather appeared on the fifth season of *Dancing with the Stars*; his partner was Ukrainian-American professional ballroom dancer Karina Smirnoff. On October 16, 2007, Smirnoff and Mayweather were the fourth couple to be eliminated from the competition, finishing in ninth place.

Personal life

Mayweather resides in a 22,000-square-foot (2,000 m^2), five-bedroom, seven-bath custom-built mansion in the Las Vegas Valley.

In 2008, Mayweather recorded a rap song titled "Yep" that he used for his entrance on WrestleMania XXIV in his match against Big Show.

Mayweather owns a boxing gym called the "Mayweather Boxing Club" located in the Chinatown Plaza in Las Vegas.

In 2011, Mayweather paid for the funeral of former super lightweight world champion and former opponent Genaro Hernandez, who died of cancer after a three-year battle.

On September 9, 2014, Mayweather announced that he would retire in 2015, doing so after defeating Andre Berto in a bout that was the last as part of his six-fight deal with the Showtime network. He enjoys spending his free time holidaying in Dubai.[1]

On May 16, 2016, it was reported on TMZ.com that Mayweather spends $1,000 on a haircut at least two times a week. TMZ spoke to Jackie Starr, the woman behind the haircuts, who states she met Floyd in 2001 but only started cutting his hair in 2009 and is the only barber to do so since whether in the US or abroad, "It's $1,000 per cut. I cut his hair two times a week, three times is pushing it, but then it also depends on the occasion. If he's in training I will cut him Monday, Wednesday and Friday."

Controversies

Criminal convictions

In 2002, Mayweather was charged with two counts of domestic violence and one count of misdemeanor battery. He received a six-month suspended sentence and two days of house arrest and was ordered to perform 48 hours of community service.

In 2004, Mayweather was given a one-year suspended jail sentence, ordered to undergo counseling for "impulse control" and pay a $1,000 fine (or perform 100 hours of community service) after being convicted of two counts of misdemeanor battery against two women.

In 2005, Mayweather pleaded no contest to a misdemeanor battery charge after hitting and kicking a bouncer, receiving a 90-day suspended jail sentence.

On September 9, 2010, it was reported that Mayweather was being sought by police for questioning after his former girlfriend, Josie Harris, filed a domestic battery report against him. Harris accused Mayweather of battery in the past, but those charges were dropped in July 2005 after Harris testified that she had lied and that Mayweather had not battered her. Mayweather was taken into custody September 10, 2010, but was released after posting $3,000 bail. Mayweather was initially charged with felony theft (stemming from the disappearance of Harris's mobile phone); on September 16 two felony coercion charges, one felony robbery charge, one misdemeanor domestic-battery charge and three misdemeanor harassment charges were added.

On December 21, 2011, a judge sentenced Mayweather to serve 90 days in the county jail for battery upon Harris in September 2010. Mayweather reached a deal with prosecutors in which he pleaded guilty to misdemeanor battery in exchange for prosecutors dropping the felony battery charge. Mayweather also pleaded no contest to two counts of misdemeanor harassment, stemming from threats to his children. In addition to the 90-day sentence Mayweather was ordered to complete 100 hours of community service, a 12-month domestic-violence program and to pay a fine of $2,500. On June 1 Mayweather began serving his county jail sentence, and was released in August 2012.

Sued for defamation

In May 2015, following his bout against Pacquiao, Josie Harris sued Mayweather for $20 million for defamation, claiming that Mayweather lied during an interview with Katie Couric in April. During that interview, he called her a drug abuser while discussing the 2010 domestic-violence incident which ended up with Mayweather going to jail for two months.

Stripped of WBO welterweight title

On Monday July 6, 2015, Floyd Mayweather was stripped of his WBO Welterweight Champion (147 lbs) title for noncompliance with the regulations of the organization. Floyd won the WBO Welterweight title when he beat Manny Pacquiao on the historic May 2 bout. However, the WBO rules say that boxers cannot hold world titles in multiple weight classes, and Floyd already held two junior middleweight championship titles when he won the welterweight title.

Floyd had until 4:30 p.m. EST on July 3 to vacate the two other belts and pay a $200,000 sanctioning fee (from the fight where Floyd was paid $220 million.) Floyd did not comply, and the WBO vacated the title on July 6, 2015.

Professional boxing record

Professional record summary [hide]		
49 fights	**49 wins**	**0 losses**
By knockout	26	0
By decision	23	0

No.	Result	Record	Opponent	Type	Round, time	Date	Location	Notes
50	N/A	N/A	Conor McGregor	N/A	– (12)	Aug 26, 2017	T-Mobile Arena, Paradise, Nevada, U.S.	
49	Win	49–0	Andre Berto	UD	12	Sep 12, 2015	MGM Grand Garden Arena, Paradise, Nevada, U.S.	Retained WBA (Super), WBC, *The Ring*, and lineal welterweight titles
48	Win	48–0	Manny Pacquiao	UD	12	May 2, 2015	MGM Grand Garden Arena, Paradise, Nevada, U.S.	Retained WBA (Super), WBC, *The Ring*, and lineal welterweight titles; Won WBO welterweight title
47	Win	47–0	Marcos Maidana	UD	12	Sep 13, 2014	MGM Grand Garden Arena, Paradise, Nevada, U.S.	Retained WBA (Super), WBC, *The Ring*, and lineal welterweight titles; Retained WBC light middleweight title
46	Win	46–0	Marcos Maidana	MD	12	May 3, 2014	MGM Grand Garden Arena, Paradise, Nevada, U.S.	Retained WBC, *The Ring*, and lineal welterweight

44

#	Result	Record	Opponent	Type	Round, time	Date	Location	Notes
45	Win	45–0	Canelo Álvarez	MD	12	Sep 14, 2013	MGM Grand Garden Arena, Paradise, Nevada, U.S.	titles; Won WBA (Super) welterweight title
44	Win	44–0	Robert Guerrero	UD	12	May 4, 2013	MGM Grand Garden Arena, Paradise, Nevada, U.S.	Retained WBA (Super) light middleweight title; Won WBC, *The Ring*, and vacant lineal light middleweight titles
43	Win	43–0	Miguel Cotto	UD	12	May 5, 2012	MGM Grand Garden Arena, Paradise, Nevada, U.S.	Retained WBC and lineal welterweight titles; Won vacant *The Ring* welterweight title
42	Win	42–0	Victor Ortiz	KO	4 (12), 2:59	Sep 17, 2011	MGM Grand Garden Arena, Paradise, Nevada, U.S.	Won WBA (Super) light middleweight title
41	Win	41–0	Shane Mosley	UD	12	May 1, 2010	MGM Grand Garden Arena, Paradise, Nevada, U.S.	Retained lineal welterweight title; Won WBC welterweight title
40	Win	40–0	Juan Manuel Márquez	UD	12	Sep 19, 2009	MGM Grand Garden Arena, Paradise, Nevada, U.S.	Won lineal welterweight title

39	Win	39–0	🇬🇧Ricky Hatton	TKO	10 (12), 1:35	Dec 8, 2007	🇺🇸MGM Grand Garden Arena, Paradise, Nevada, U.S.	Retained WBC, *The Ring*, and lineal welterweight titles
38	Win	38–0	🇺🇸Oscar De La Hoya	SD	12	May 5, 2007	🇺🇸MGM Grand Garden Arena, Paradise, Nevada, U.S.	Won WBC light middleweight title
37	Win	37–0	🇦🇷Carlos Baldomir	UD	12	Nov 4, 2006	🇺🇸Mandalay Bay Events Center, Paradise, Nevada, U.S.	Retained IBO welterweight title; Won WBC, IBA, *The Ring*, and lineal welterweight titles
36	Win	36–0	🇺🇸Zab Judah	UD	12	Apr 8, 2006	🇺🇸Thomas & Mack Center, Paradise, Nevada, U.S.	Won IBF and vacant IBO welterweight titles
35	Win	35–0	🇺🇸Sharmba Mitchell	TKO	6 (12), 2:06	Nov 19, 2005	🇺🇸Rose Garden, Portland, Oregon, U.S.	
34	Win	34–0	🇨🇦Arturo Gatti	RTD	6 (12), 3:00	Jun 25, 2005	🇺🇸Boardwalk Hall, Atlantic City, New Jersey, U.S.	Won WBC super lightweight title
33	Win	33–0	🇵🇷Henry Bruseles	TKO	8 (12), 2:55	Jan 22, 2005	🇺🇸American Airlines Arena, Miami, Florida, U.S.	
32	Win	32–0	🇺🇸DeMarcus Corley	UD	12	May 22, 2004	🇺🇸Boardwalk Hall, Atlantic City, New Jersey, U.S.	
31	Win	31–0	🇿🇦Phillip N'dou	TKO	7 (12), 1:08	Nov 1,	🇺🇸Van Andel Arena, Grand Rapids,	Retained WBC, *The Ring*, and

						2003	Michigan, U.S.	lineal lightweight titles
30	Win	30–0	Victoriano Sosa	UD	12	Apr 19, 2003	Selland Arena, Fresno, California, U.S.	Retained WBC, *The Ring*, and lineal lightweight titles
29	Win	29–0	José Luis Castillo	UD	12	Dec 7, 2002	Mandalay Bay Events Center, Paradise, Nevada, U.S.	Retained WBC, *The Ring*, and lineal lightweight titles
28	Win	28–0	José Luis Castillo	UD	12	Apr 20, 2002	MGM Grand Garden Arena, Paradise, Nevada, U.S.	Won WBC, vacant *The Ring* and lineal lightweight titles
27	Win	27–0	Jesús Chávez	RTD	9 (12), 3:00	Nov 10, 2001	Bill Graham Civic Auditorium, San Francisco, California, U.S.	Retained WBC and lineal super featherweight titles
26	Win	26–0	Carlos Hernández	UD	12	May 26, 2001	Van Andel Arena, Grand Rapids, Michigan, U.S.	Retained WBC and lineal super featherweight titles
25	Win	25–0	Diego Corrales	TKO	10 (12), 2:19	Jan 20, 2001	MGM Grand Garden Arena, Paradise, Nevada, U.S.	Retained WBC and lineal super featherweight titles
24	Win	24–0	Emanuel Augustus	TKO	9 (10), 1:06	Oct 21, 2000	Cobo Hall, Detroit, Michigan, U.S.	
23	Win	23–0	Gregorio Vargas	UD	12	Mar 18, 2000	MGM Grand Garden Arena, Paradise, Nevada, U.S.	Retained WBC and lineal super featherweight titles

47

22	Win	22–0	🇨🇺 Carlos Gerena	RTD	7 (12), 3:00	Sep 11, 1999	Mandalay Bay Events Center, Paradise, Nevada, U.S.	Retained WBC and lineal super featherweight titles
21	Win	21–0	Justin Juuko	KO	9 (12), 1:20	May 22, 1999	Mandalay Bay Events Center, Paradise, Nevada, U.S.	Retained WBC and lineal super featherweight titles
20	Win	20–0	Carlos Rios	UD	12	Feb 17, 1999	Van Andel Arena, Grand Rapids, Michigan, U.S.	Retained WBC and lineal super featherweight titles
19	Win	19–0	Angel Manfredy	TKO	2 (12), 2:47	Dec 19, 1998	Miccosukee Resort and Gaming, Miami, Florida, U.S.	Retained WBC and lineal super featherweight titles
18	Win	18–0	Genaro Hernández	RTD	8 (12), 3:00	Oct 3, 1998	Las Vegas Hilton, Winchester, Nevada, U.S.	Won WBC and lineal super featherweight titles
17	Win	17–0	Tony Pep	UD	10	Jun 14, 1998	Etess Arena, Atlantic City, New Jersey, U.S.	
16	Win	16–0	Gustavo Cuello	UD	10	Apr 18, 1998	Grand Olympic Auditorium, Los Angeles, California, U.S.	
15	Win	15–0	Miguel Melo	TKO	3 (10), 2:30	Mar 23, 1998	Foxwoods Resort Casino, Ledyard, Connecticut, U.S.	
14	Win	14–0	Sam Girard	KO	2 (10), 2:47	Feb 28,	Bally's, Atlantic City,

							1998	New Jersey, U.S.
13	Win	13–0	🇵🇷 Hector Arroyo	TKO	5 1:21	(10),	Jan 9, 1998	🇺🇸 Grand Casino, Biloxi, Mississippi, U.S.
12	Win	12–0	🇺🇸 Angelo Nuñez	TKO	3 2:42	(8),	Nov 20, 1997	🇺🇸 Grand Olympic Auditorium, Los Angeles, California, U.S.
11	Win	11–0	🇺🇸 Felipe Garcia	KO	6 2:56	(8),	Oct 14, 1997	🇺🇸 Qwest Arena, Boise, Idaho, U.S.
10	Win	10–0	🇺🇸 Louie Leija	TKO	2 2:33	(10),	Sep 6, 1997	🇺🇸 County Coliseum, El Paso, Texas, U.S.
9	Win	9–0	🇺🇸 Jesús Chávez	TKO	5 2:02	(6),	Jul 12, 1997	🇺🇸 Grand Casino, Biloxi, Mississippi, U.S.
8	Win	8–0	🇺🇸 Larry O'Shields	UD	6		Jun 14, 1997	🇺🇸 Alamodome, San Antonio, Texas, U.S.
7	Win	7–0	🇺🇸 Tony Duran	TKO	1 1:12	(6),	May 9, 1997	🇺🇸 The Orleans, Paradise, Nevada, U.S.
6	Win	6–0	🇺🇸 Bobby Giepert	TKO	1 1:30	(6),	Apr 12, 1997	🇺🇸 Thomas & Mack Center, Paradise, Nevada, U.S.
5	Win	5–0	🇺🇸 Kino Rodriguez	TKO	1 1:44	(6),	Mar 12, 1997	🇺🇸 DeltaPlex Arena, Walker, Michigan, U.S.
4	Win	4–0	🇺🇸 Edgar Ayala	TKO	2 1:39	(4),	Feb 1,	🇺🇸 Swiss Park Hall, Chula Vista,

						1997	California, U.S.	
3	Win	3–0	Jerry Cooper	TKO	1 1:39 (4),	Jan 18, 1997	Thomas & Mack Center, Paradise, Nevada, U.S.	
2	Win	2–0	Reggie Sanders	UD	4	Nov 30, 1996	Tingley Coliseum, Albuquerque, New Mexico, U.S.	
1	Win	1–0	Roberto Apodaca	TKO	2 0:37 (4),	Oct 11, 1996	Texas Station, North Las Vegas, Nevada, U.S.	Professional debut

Titles in boxing

Major world titles

- WBC super featherweight champion (130 lbs)
- WBC lightweight champion (135 lbs)
- WBC super lightweight champion (140 lbs)
- IBF welterweight champion (147 lbs)
- WBC welterweight champion (2×)
- WBC light middleweight champion (154 lbs) (2×)
- WBA (Super) light middleweight champion
- WBA (Super) welterweight champion
- WBO welterweight champion

Minor world titles

- IBO welterweight champion
- IBA welterweight champion

***The Ring* magazine titles**

- *The Ring* lightweight champion
- *The Ring* welterweight champion (2×)

- *The Ring* light middleweight champion

Lineal titles

- Lineal super featherweight champion
- Lineal lightweight champion
- Lineal welterweight champion (2×)
- Lineal light middleweight champion

Honorary titles

- WBC All Africa super lightweight champion[
- WBC Emeritus light middleweight champion
- WBC Diamond light middleweight champion
- WBC 24K Gold light middleweight champion[
- WBC Supreme light middleweight champion
- WBC $1,000,000 Emerald welterweight champion
- WBA Man of Triumph Gold welterweight champion

Pay-per-view bouts

No.	Date	Fight	Billing	Buys	Network	Revenue
1	June 25, 2005	**Gatti** vs. **Mayweather**	Thunder & Lightning	365,000	HBO	$16,500,000
2	April 8, 2006	**Mayweather** vs. **Judah**	Sworn Enemies	374,000	HBO	$16,800,000
3	November 4, 2006	**Mayweather** vs. **Baldomir**	Pretty Risky	325,000	HBO	$16,300,000
4	May 5, 2007	**De La Hoya** vs. **Mayweather**	The World Awaits	2,400,000[205]	HBO	$136,000,000
5	December 8, 2007	**Mayweather** vs. **Hatton**	Undefeated	920,000	HBO	$50,000,000
6	September	**Mayweather**	Number One/Número	1,100,000[206]	HBO	$55,600,000

	19, 2009	vs. **Márquez**	Uno			
7	May 1, 2010	**Mayweather** vs. **Mosley**	Who R U Picking?	1,400,000[207]	HBO	$78,300,000
8	September 17, 2011	**Mayweather** vs. **Ortiz**	Star Power	1,250,000[208]	HBO	$78,440,000
9	May 5, 2012	**Mayweather** vs. **Cotto**	Ring Kings	1,500,000[209]	HBO	$94,000,000
10	May 4, 2013	**Mayweather** vs. **Guerrero**	May Day	1,000,000[210]	Showtime	$60,000,000
11	September 14, 2013	**Mayweather** vs. **Canelo**	The One	2,200,000[211]	Showtime	$150,000,000
12	May 3, 2014	**Mayweather** vs. **Maidana**	The Moment	900,000[212]	Showtime	$58,000,000
13	September 13, 2014	**Mayweather** vs. **Maidana** II	Mayhem	925,000[213]	Showtime	$60,000,000
14	May 2, 2015	**Mayweather** vs. **Pacquiao**	Fight of the Century	4,600,000[214]	Showtime/HBO	$400,000,000
15	September 12, 2015	**Mayweather** vs. **Berto**	High Stakes	400,000[215]	Showtime	$28,000,000
16	August 26, 2017	**Mayweather** vs. **McGregor**	The Money Fight		Showtime	

Totals (approximate): 19,500,000 buys and $1,300,000,000 in revenue.

Filmography

Films

Year	Series	Role	Notes
2003	*More than Famous*	Himself	
2007	*The World Awaits: De La Hoya vs. Mayweather*	Himself	Documentary
2014	*Think Like a Man Too*	Himself	Cameo appearance

Television series

Year	Series	Role	Notes
2005	*Countdown to Gatti-Mayweather*	Himself	Documentary
2006	*Soul of a Champion*	Himself	Documentary
	Countdown to Baldomir-Mayweather	Himself	Documentary
2007	*24/7: De La Hoya/Mayweather*	Himself	
	24/7: Mayweather/Hatton	Himself	
2009	*Countdown to Mayweather–Marquez*	Himself	Documentary
	24/7: Mayweather/Marquez	Himself	
2010	*24/7: Mayweather/Mosley*	Himself	
2011	*24/7: Mayweather/Ortiz*	Himself	
2012	*24/7: Mayweather/Cotto*	Himself	
	Ridiculousness	Himself	Season 2, Episode 2
	30 Days In May	Himself	Documentary
2013	*Mayweather*	Himself	Documentary
	All Access: Mayweather vs. Guerrero	Himself	
	All Access: Mayweather vs. Canelo	Himself	

	All Access: Mayweather vs. Maidana	Himself	
2014			
	All Access: Mayweather vs. Maidana II	Himself	
	Inside Mayweather vs. Pacquiao	Himself	Documentary
2015	*At Last: Mayweather vs. Pacquiao*	Himself	Documentary
	All Access: Mayweather vs. Berto	Himself	

Video Games

Year	Title	Role	Notes
1999	*Knockout Kings 2000*	Himself	Playable fighter
2000	*Knockout Kings 2001*	Himself	Playable fighter
2002	*Knockout Kings 2002*	Himself	Playable fighter
2002	*Knockout Kings 2003*	Himself	Playable fighter
2005	*Fight Night Round 2*	Himself	Playable fighter

Honors and awards

- 1993 Michigan State Golden Gloves Champion, 106 Lbs[
- 1993 National Golden Gloves Champion, 106 Lbs[
- 1994 Michigan State Golden Gloves Champion, 112 Lbs
- 1994 National Golden Gloves Champion, 112 Lbs; Outstanding Boxer Award[
- 1995 National PAL Champion, 125 Lbs; Outstanding Boxer Award
- 1995 United States national amateur boxing featherweight champions, 125 Lbs
- 1995 Competed at Featherweight at the World Amateur Boxing Championships
- 1996 Michigan State Golden Gloves Champion, 125 Lbs[]
- 1996 National Golden Gloves Champion, 125 Lbs
- 1996 Qualified as a Featherweight for the United States Olympic Team
- 1996 Atlanta Olympics Featherweight Bronze medalist

- 1998 and 2007 International Boxing Award Fighter of the Year
- 1998 and 2007 *The Ring* Magazine Fighter of the Year
- 2002 World Boxing Hall of Fame Fighter of the Year
- 2005 and 2007 World Boxing Council Boxer of the Year
- 2005–08 *The Ring* 'number one' pound for pound
- 2007 Boxing Writers Association of America Fighter of the Year
- 2007 ESPN Fighter of the Year[
- 2007 *Forbes* Magazine, Ranked "Number 14" Richest Celebrity Paydays
- 2007 *New York Daily News* Fighter of the Year
- 2007 World Boxing Council Event of the Year (The World Awaits)
- 2007 World Boxing Council Knockout of the Year (against Ricky Hatton)
- 2007, 2008 and 2010 Best Fighter ESPY Award
- 2007, 2008 and 2010 *The Ring* Magazine Event of the Year
- 2008 *Sports Illustrated*, The 50 Highest-Earning American Athletes (ranked 4th)
- 2008 Yahoo Sports, Ranked "Number 6" Most Powerful People in Boxing[
- 2009 *The Ring* Magazine Comeback of the Year
- 2009–10 BoxRec, BBC Sport and Yahoo! Sports 'number one' pound for pound
- 2010 Yahoo! Sports Boxing's Most Influential (ranked 70th)
- 2010 *Forbes* magazine Celebrity 100 (ranked 31st)
- 2010 *Forbes* Magazine, The World's 50 Top-Earning Athletes (ranked 2nd)
- 2010 *Sports Illustrated*, The 50 Highest-Earning American Athletes (ranked 3rd)
- 2012 *Forbes* Magazine #1 of the world's 100 highest paid athletes.
- 2012 *Sports Illustrated* #1 fortunes 50.[
- 2012 Best Fighter ESPY Award
- 2013 *The Ring* 'number one' pound for pound.
- 2013 Boxing Writers Association of America Fighter of the Year
- 2015 *The Best Ever Award*.
- 2015 Forbes, Ranked "Number One" as The World's Highest-Paid Celebrities.
- 2015 Boxing Writers Association of America Fighter of the Year
- 2016 Guinness World Records Most bouts undefeated by a world champion boxer in a career (49)
- 2016 Guinness World Records Highest career pay-per-view sales for a boxer ($1.3 billion)
- 2016 Guinness World Records Most expensive boxing championship belt ($1 Million)

Made in the USA
Coppell, TX
23 April 2021